Popcorn
ELT
Readers

Meet ...
everyone from

Hi, I'm Po. I'm very good at kung fu. I'm the Dragon Warrior.

Hello, I'm Po's dad. I cook noodles.

Po's dad

Po

I'm Master Shifu. I live at the Jade Palace. I'm Po's teacher.

Master Shifu

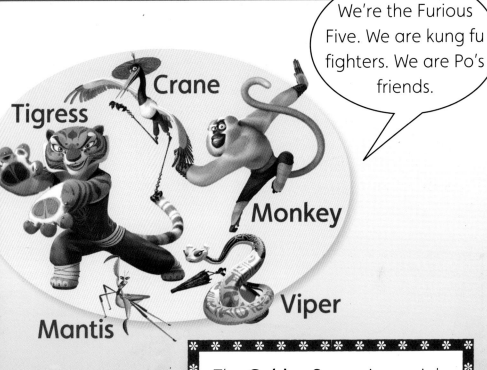

Tigress

Crane

Monkey

Viper

Mantis

We're the Furious Five. We are kung fu fighters. We are Po's friends.

The **Golden Spoon** is special. The Dragon Warrior gives it to a cook at Winter Festival. He cooks dinner at the Palace.

I'm Wo Hop. I'm a rabbit. I'm a cook too.

The Golden Spoon

Wo Hop

Before you read ...
What do you think?
Is Po a good cook?

New Words

What do these new words mean? Ask your teacher or use your dictionary.

decorations

There are a lot of **decorations**.

choose

He is **choosing** a fish.

family

This is a **family**.

cook / a cook

He's **cooking** an egg.
He's a **cook**.

festival

This is a **festival**.

fight/ a fighter

The girls are **fighting**.
They are good **fighters**.

special

He's got a **special** drink.

food

noodles

There's a lot of **food**.

winter

It's **winter**. It's cold!

I've got an idea!

I've got an idea!

What does the title *Kung Fu Panda Holiday* mean? Ask your teacher.

help

He's **helping** his mother.

CHAPTER ONE
Winter Festival is here!

It's Winter Festival. Po and his dad are very happy.

'I love Winter Festival,' Po says.

'Me too!' his dad says. 'Let's put up the decorations.'

Master Shifu goes to Po's home.

'At Winter Festival, the Dragon Warrior gives a dinner at the Jade Palace. You choose the cook!' Master Shifu says.

'Wow!' Po says. 'Can my dad come to the dinner?'

'No,' says Master Shifu. 'It's for the special kung fu teachers.'

Po is not very happy.

Po sees the Furious Five. 'I'm giving a special dinner at the Palace,' he says.

His friends laugh. 'You?' they ask.

'Yes, me. I'm the Dragon Warrior,' Po says.

CHAPTER TWO
The Golden Spoon

There are many cooks at the Jade Palace.

'I choose the cook,' Po says. 'I give the Golden Spoon to him.'

The cooks want the Golden Spoon. The first cook is Wo Hop.

Suddenly Po sees Monkey from the Furious Five. He stands up. 'Hello, Monkey,' he says.

Everyone looks at Po. 'The Dragon Warrior doesn't like Wo Hop's food!' they say.

Wo Hop is angry.

'I've got an idea!' Po thinks. 'My dad can cook the Palace dinner.'

Po eats the cooks' food but now he doesn't want it. 'Thank you, but my answer is no!' he says to the cooks.

The cooks go home.

Po goes home too. He gives the Golden Spoon to his dad. 'You are the cook at the Palace dinner!' he says.

Po's dad is very happy. 'When is the dinner?' he asks.

'Tomorrow,' says Po.

'No!' his dad says. 'At Winter Festival I always cook dinner here for family and friends.'

Po is very sad.

CHAPTER THREE
Kung fu in the kitchen

'Now we don't have a cook for the dinner!'
Master Shifu says.

'It's OK,' Po says. 'I can cook.'

Po is cooking in the kitchen. He is having a lot of problems with the special dinner. Suddenly Wo Hop comes in. 'You don't like my food!' he says. He is angry.

'You are a good cook. Please help me!' Po says.

'No!' Wo Hop says. 'I'm here to fight you!'

Po stops him. 'Help me first!' he says.

'OK,' says Wo Hop.

The Furious Five come into the kitchen.
'Please help me!' Po says.
The Furious Five put the food on the
table with some special kung fu. Zap! Pow!

The kung fu teachers come to the Palace. Master Shifu sees the table. 'Very good,' he says. 'Let's start the dinner.'

Everyone sits down. Po is sad because his dad is not there.

CHAPTER FOUR
Winter Festival at Po's house

Everyone is quiet. They look at Po.

'I'm going home now,' says Po.

'I don't understand,' Master Shifu says.

'Winter Festival is for family,' Po answers.

Po goes. The kung fu teachers start to talk. 'Yes, Winter Festival is important for families,' they say. 'You can laugh and dance and sing.'

Now they are not happy at the Palace dinner.

Po is at home. He helps his father. His family and friends are there. Everyone is happy.

Wo Hop and the kung fu teachers go to Po's house. 'This is good,' the teachers say.
Po gives the Golden Spoon to Wo Hop. 'Thank you for your help,' he says.

Master Shifu goes to Po's house. Everyone is laughing.

'Now I understand,' Master Shifu says. 'Winter Festival is for family and friends.'

'Come in,' Po says.

'Thank you!' Master Shifu says. 'This Winter Festival is good!'

THE END

Winter Festivals

Father Christmas

In many countries there are festivals in winter.

Christmas Day

Christmas Day is on the 25th of December. At Christmas, families have a tree at home. They put decorations on the tree and presents under it. There is a big family dinner. People give presents and write cards to friends. Children sometimes write to Father Christmas and ask for presents.

★ **Did you know?** The day before Christmas is 'Christmas Eve' i English. ★

tree

present

Dong Zhi

Dong Zhi is a winter festival in China. It is in December. Some families have a special dinner and eat 'tang yuan'.

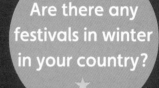
China

Tang yuan

Are there any festivals in winter in your country?

A Chinese family celebrate New Year.

Chinese New Year

For Chinese New Year people put up red decorations. There is a big family dinner and people see friends too. Children receive money in red envelopes.

What do these words mean? Find out.
people card receive money envelope

After you read

1 Read the sentences. Write a name.

Master Shifu   Po   Wo Hop   Po's dad

a) He wants the Golden Spoon. ....**Wo Hop**........

b) He can't go to the dinner at the Palace.

....

c) He doesn't understand Po. ....

d) He fights Po. ....

e) He helps his dad. ....

f) He helps Po in the kitchen. ....

2 Yes or No? Read and circle.

a) Master Shifu goes to Po's house.   (Yes) / No

b) You can dance at the Palace dinner.   Yes / No

c) Po can choose the cook.   Yes / No

d) Wo Hop is angry with Po.   Yes / No

e) Po is happy at the Palace dinner.   Yes / No

Where's the popcorn?
Look in your book.
Can you find it?

Puzzle time!

1 Look and match. What are the presents?
Choose from the words in the box.

| computer pen car ball bag book |

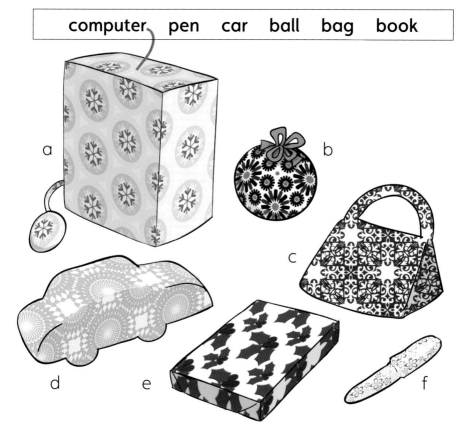

a   b   c   d   e   f

2 Can you find five more words in the noodles?

3 Look at the pictures and write the words.

1 n o o d l e s

2 ... o o ...

3 ... ... o o ...

4 ... o o ...

5 ... o o ...

6 S ... ... o o ...

4 Draw your family dinner. Write the names and complete the sentences. Show your picture to your friends.

This is my family. We eat ....

We drink ....

Imagine ...

Work with a friend. Act out the scenes.

A **Master Shifu:** At Winter Festival, the Dragon Warrior gives a dinner at the Jade Palace. You choose the cook.

Po: Wow! Can my dad come? Can we dance and sing?

Master Shifu: No! Your dad can't come. You can't dance or sing. It's a special dinner!

Po: But I'm always with my dad at Winter Festival.

B **Wo Hop:** I'm angry because you don't like my food.

Po: You are a good cook. Can you help?

Wo Hop: No! I'm here to fight!

Po: Help me first! Please!

Wo Hop: OK.

Chant

1 **Listen and read.**

Kung Fu Panda holiday!

There's a dinner at the Palace
But the Dragon Warrior's sad.
He cooks for kung fu teachers
But he can't be with his dad.
'The dinner's good, but now I see
The festival's for family.'
'Goodbye,' he says. 'See you soon.'
He gives Wo Hop the Golden Spoon.
'Come in! Come in! Let's sing and play,
It's a Kung Fu Panda holiday!

2 **Say the chant.**